Peter Ilyich
TCHAIKOVSKY

MARCHE SLAVE
Op. 31
Edited by
Richard W. Sargeant, Jr.

Study Score
Partitur

SERENISSIMA MUSIC, INC.

ORCHESTRA

2 Piccolos

2 Flutes

2 Oboes

2 Clarinets (B-flat)

2 Bassoons

4 Horns (F)

2 Trumpets (C)*

2 Cornets (B-flat)

3 Trombones

Tuba

Timpani

Percussion

Snare Drum, Bass Drum/Cymbal

Harp

Violin I

Violin II

Viola

Violoncello

Double Bass

*The present score has been updated for the common keys of modern instruments
(Clarinets in A or B-flat, Horns in F, Trumpets in C). The original score featured
Trumpets in B-flat.

Duration: ca. 10 minutes

Premiere: November 18, 1876
Moscow, Russia
Russian Musical Society
RMS Orchestra / Nikolay Rubinstein

ISMN: 979-0-58042-115-9
This score is a newly engraved edition prepared from primary sources;
including the composer's holograph and the first efition score and parts
issued by P. Jurgenson of Moscow in between 1879 and 1891, including
the revisions included in the 1891 full score.

Printed in the USA
First Printing: August, 2018

SLAVONIC MARCH
Op. 31

Pyotr Tchaikovsky
Edited by Richard W. Sargeant, Jr.

Moderato in modo di marcia funebre

Moderato in modo di marcia funebre

42271

7
Picc. 1 2
Fl. 1 2
Ob. 1 2
Cl. 1 2
Bn. 1 2
Hn. 1 2 3 4
Tpt. 1 2
Cor. 1 2
Trb. 1 2
Bass Tuba
Timp.
S. D. T.-t.
Cymb. B. D.
7
Vn. 1 2
Va.
Vc.
Cb.

13
Picc. 1 2
a2
Fl. 1 2
p espress.
Ob. 1 2
1.
Cl. 1 2
p espress.
Bn. 1 2
p
2.
Hn. 1 2
p poco marc.
3 4
Tpt. 1 2
Cor. 1 2
1.
Trb. 1 2
p poco marc.
Bass Tuba
Timp.
p
S. D.
T.-t.
Cymb.
B. D.
pp
13
Vn. 1
p piangendo (lamenting)
2
p piangendo (lamenting)
pizz.
Va.
p
pizz.
Vc.
p
pizz.
Cb.
p

19
Picc. 1 2
Fl. 1 2
p espress. e sensíbile (with feeling)
Ob. 1 2
a2
p espress. e sensíbile (with feeling)
Cl. 1 2
p
Bn. 1 2
1.
Hn. 1 2
p
a2
3 4
p
Tpt. 1 2
Cor. 1 2
Trb. 1 2
Bass Tuba
Timp.
S. D. T.-t.
Cymb. B. D.
19
Vn. 1
p
2
p
Va.
arco
p piangendo (lamenting)
p
Vc.
arco
p piangendo (lamenting)
p
Cb.
arco

25
29
Picc. 1 2
Fl. 1 2
mf con dolcezza
Ob. 1 2
1.
mf con dolcezza
Cl. 1 2
mf
Bn. 1 2
mf
1.
2.
Hn. 1 2
p
mf
Hn. 3 4
4.
p
Tpt. 1 2
Cor. 1 2
mf
Trb. 1 2
Bass Tuba
Timp.
S. D. T.-t.
p
Cymb. B. D.
29
25
Vn. 1
mf con dolcezza
Vn. 2
mf con dolcezza
Va.
poco più f
pizz.
mf
Vc.
poco più f
pizz.
mf
Cb.
pizz.
mf

30
Picc. 1 2
Fl. 1 2
Ob. 1 2
Cl. 1 2
Bn. 1 2
Hn. 1 2
3 4
mf
Tpt. 1 2
mf
Cor. 1 2
Trb. 1 2
Bass Tuba
Timp.
S. D. T.-t.
Cymb. B. D.
30
Vn. 1
2
Va.
Vc.
Cb.

34
Picc. 1 2
Fl. 1 2
Ob. 1 2
Cl. 1 2
Bn. 1 2
a2
Hn. 1 2 3 4
3.
Tpt. 1 2
Cor. 1 2
Trb. 1 2
B. T.
Bass Tuba
Timp.
S. D. T.-t.
Cymb. B. D.
34
Vn. 1 2
Va.
Vc.
Cb.
arco
pizz.

38
Picc. 1 2
Fl. 1 2
Ob. 1 2
Cl. 1 2
Bn. 1 2
a2
Hn. 1 2 3 4
Tpt. 1 2
Cor. 1 2
Trb. 1 2
Bass Tuba
Timp.
S. D. T.-t.
Cymb. B. D.
Vn. 1 2
Va.
Vc.
Cb.

41
Picc. 1 2
Fl. 1 2
cresc. poco a poco
Ob. 1 2
cresc. poco a poco
Cl. 1 2
a2
cresc. poco a poco
Bn. 1 2
cresc. poco a poco
Hn. 1 2
p
a2
Hn. 3 4
Tpt. 1 2
1.
a2
p
Cor. 1 2
Trb. 1 2
Bass Tuba
Tuba
p cresc. poco a poco
Timp.
cresc. poco a poco
S. D. T.-t.
p cresc. poco a poco
Cymb. B. D.
41
Vn. 1
cresc. poco a poco
Vn. 2
cresc. poco a poco
Va.
arco
cresc. poco a poco
Vc.
arco
cresc. poco a poco
Cb.
cresc. poco a poco

44
Picc. 1 2
Fl. 1 2
Ob. 1 2
Cl. 1 2
Bn. 1 2
Hn. 1 2 3 4
Tpt. 1 2
Cor. 1 2
Trb. 1 2
Bass Tuba
Timp.
S. D. T.-t.
Cymb. B. D.
Vn. 1 2
Va.
Vc.
Cb.
mf
più f

47
Picc. 1 2
Fl. 1 2
Ob. 1 2
Cl. 1 2
Bn. 1 2
Hn. 1 2 3 4
Tpt. 1 2
Cor. 1 2
Trb. 1 2
Bass Tuba
Timp.
S. D. T.-t.
Cymb. B. D.
Vn. 1 2
Va.
Vc.
Cb.
2.
3.
a2
pizz.
arco
f
sf
mf

50
Picc. 1 2
Fl. 1 2
cresc.
Ob. 1 2
2.
cresc.
Cl. 1 2
cresc.
Bn. 1 2
cresc.
Hn. 1 2
a2
3 4
Tpt. 1 2
f
Cor. 1 2
f
a2
Trb. 1 2
f
Bass Tuba
f
Timp.
f
S. D. T.-t.
fp
Cymb. B. D.
50
Vn. 1
cresc.
2
cresc.
Va.
arco
cresc.
Vc.
arco
Cb.

53
Picc. 1 2
Fl. 1 2
ff
Ob. 1 2
Cl. 1 2
Bn. 1 2
Hn. 1 2 3 4
Tpt. 1 2
Cor. 1 2
Trb. 1 2
Bass Tuba
Timp.
S. D. T.-t.
Cymb. B. D.
Vn. 1 2
Va.
Vc.
Cb.

58
56
a2
Picc. 1 2
ff
Fl. 1 2
ff
Ob. 1 2
a2
ff marc.
Cl. 1 2
ff
Bn. 1 2
ff
Hn. 1 2 3 4
a2
ff marc.
a2
ff
Tpt. 1 2
a2
ff marc.
Cor. 1 2
ff
Trb. 1 2
ff
Bass Tuba
ff
Timp.
ff
S. D. T.-t.
ff
Cymb. B. D.
58
56
Vn. 1 2
Va.
Vc.
marc.
Cb.

59
Picc. 1 2
Fl. 1 2
Ob. 1 2
Cl. 1 2
Bn. 1 2
Hn. 1 2 3 4
Tpt. 1 2
Cor. 1 2
Trb. 1 2
Bass Tuba
Timp.
S. D. T.-t.
Cymb. B. D.
59
Vn. 1 2
Va.
Vc.
Cb.

62
Picc. 1 2
Fl. 1 2
Ob. 1 2
Cl. 1 2
Bn. 1 2
Hn. 1 2 3 4
Tpt. 1 2
Cor. 1 2
Trb. 1 2
Bass Tuba
Timp.
S. D. T.-t.
Cymb. B. D.
62
Vn. 1 2
Va.
Vc.
Cb.

65
Picc. 1 2
Fl. 1 2
Ob. 1 2
Cl. 1 2
Bn. 1 2
Hn. 1 2 3 4
Tpt. 1 2
Cor. 1 2
Trb. 1 2
Bass Tuba
Timp.
S. D. T.-t.
Cymb. B. D.
Vn. 1 2
Va.
Vc.
Cb.
a2
fff

70
Picc. 1 2
Fl. 1 2
Ob. 1 2
Cl. 1 2
Bn. 1 2
Hn. 1 2 3 4
Tpt. 1 2
Cor. 1 2
Trb. 1 2
Bass Tuba
Timp.
S. D. T.-t.
Cymb. B. D.
3
70
Vn. 1 2
Va.
Vc.
Cb.

75
Picc. 1 2
Fl. 1 2
Ob. 1 2
Cl. 1 2
Bn. 1 2
Hn. 1 2 3 4
f
f
Tpt. 1 2
ff
Cor. 1 2
ff
Trb. 1 2
Bass Tuba
Timp.
S. D. T.-t.
Cymb. B. D.
75
Vn. 1 2
Va.
Vc.
Cb.
pizz.
ff
f

84 L'stesso tempo

87
Picc. 1 2
Fl. 1 2
Ob. 1 2
Cl. 1 2
Bn. 1 2
Hn. 1 2 3 4
Tpt. 1 2
mp
Cor. 1 2
Trb. 1 2
mp
B. T.
p
Bass Tuba
Timp.
S. D. T.-t.
p
Cymb. B. D.
87
(pizz.)
p
Vn. 1 2
(pizz.)
p
(pizz.)
p
Va.
Vc.
Cb.

93
Picc.
Fl.
Ob.
Cl.
Bn.
Hn.
Tpt.
Cor.
Trb.
Bass Tuba
Timp.
S. D. T.-t.
Cymb. B. D.
Vn.
Va.
Vc.
Cb.
f
mf marc.
poco più f

97
98
Picc. 1 2
Fl. 1 2
Ob. 1 2
Cl. 1 2
Bn. 1 2
Hn. 1 2 3 4
Tpt. 1 2
Cor. 1 2
Trb. 1 2
Bass Tuba
Timp.
S. D. T.-t.
Cymb. B. D.
Vn. 1 2
Va.
Vc.
Cb.
a2
ff
arco

101
Picc. 1 2
Fl. 1 2
a2
Ob. 1 2
Cl. 1 2
Bn. 1 2
Hn. 1 2
3 4
Tpt. 1 2
Cor. 1 2
Trb. 1 2
Bass Tuba
Timp.
S. D. T.-t.
Cymb. B. D.
ff
101
Vn. 1
2
Va.
Vc.
Cb.

105
Picc. 1 2
Fl. 1 2
a2
a2
Ob. 1 2
Cl. 1 2
Bn. 1 2
Hn. 1 2
Hn. 3 4
Tpt. 1 2
Cor. 1 2
Trb. 1 2
Bass Tuba
Timp.
S. D. T.-t.
Cymb. B. D.
105
Vn. 1
Vn. 2
Va.
Vc.
Cb.

109
Picc. 1 2
Fl. 1 2
a2
Ob. 1 2
Cl. 1 2
Bn. 1 2
Hn. 1 2 3 4
mf marc.
Tpt. 1 2
Cor. 1 2
Trb. 1 2
Bass Tuba
Timp.
S. D. T.-t.
Cymb. B. D.
Vn. 1 2
Va.
Vc.
pizz.
poco più f
Cb.
pizz.
poco più f

113
Picc. 1 2
Fl. 1 2
Ob. 1 2
Cl. 1 2
Bn. 1 2
Hn. 1 2
3 4
Tpt. 1 2
Cor. 1 2
Trb. 1 2
Bass Tuba
Timp.
S. D. T.-t.
Cymb. B. D.
113
Vn. 1
2
Va.
Vc.
Cb.
ff
a2
arco

117
Picc. 1 2
Fl. 1 2
a2
Ob. 1 2
Cl. 1 2
Bn. 1 2
Hn. 1 2 3 4
Tpt. 1 2
Cor. 1 2
Trb. 1 2
Bass Tuba
Timp.
S. D. T.-t.
Cymb. B. D.
ff
117
Vn. 1 2
Va.
Vc.
Cb.

121
Picc. 1 2
a2
fff
Fl. 1 2
a2
fff
Ob. 1 2
a2
fff
Cl. 1 2
fff
Bn. 1 2
a2
fff
Hn. 1 2 3 4
Tpt. 1 2
ff
Cor. 1 2
ff
Trb. 1 2
Bass Tuba
Tuba
fff
Timp.
S. D. T.-t.
Cymb. B. D.
121
Vn. 1 2
fff
Va.
fff
Vc.
fff
Cb.
fff

124
Picc. 1 2
Fl. 1 2
Ob. 1 2
Cl. 1 2
Bn. 1 2
Hn. 1 2 3 4
Tpt. 1 2
Cor. 1 2
Trb. 1 2
Bass Tuba
Timp.
S. D. T.-t.
Cymb. B. D.
124
Vn. 1 2
Va.
Vc.
Cb.

127
Picc. 1 2
Fl. 1 2
Ob. 1 2
a2
Cl. 1 2
Bn. 1 2
Hn. 1 2 3 4
Tpt. 1 2
Cor. 1 2
Trb. 1 2
Bass Tuba
Timp.
S. D. T.-t.
Cymb. B. D.
127
Vn. 1 2
Va.
Vc.
Cb.

130
132
Picc. 1 2
Fl. 1 2
Ob. 1 2
Cl. 1 2
Bn. 1 2
a2
Hn. 1 2 3 4
3.
Tpt. 1 2
Cor. 1 2
Trb. 1 2
Bass Tuba
B. T.
Timp.
S. D. T.-t.
Cymb. B. D.
Vn. 1 2
Va.
Vc.
Cb.
pizz.
p

133
Picc. 1 2
Fl. 1 2
p
Ob. 1 2
a2
p
Cl. 1 2
p
Bn. 1 2
a2
p
Hn. 1 2
Hn.
3 4
Tpt. 1 2
p
Cor. 1 2
1 2
Trb.
Bass Tuba
Timp.
S. D. T.-t.
Cymb. B. D.
133
1
p
Vn.
2
Va.
Vc.
Cb.

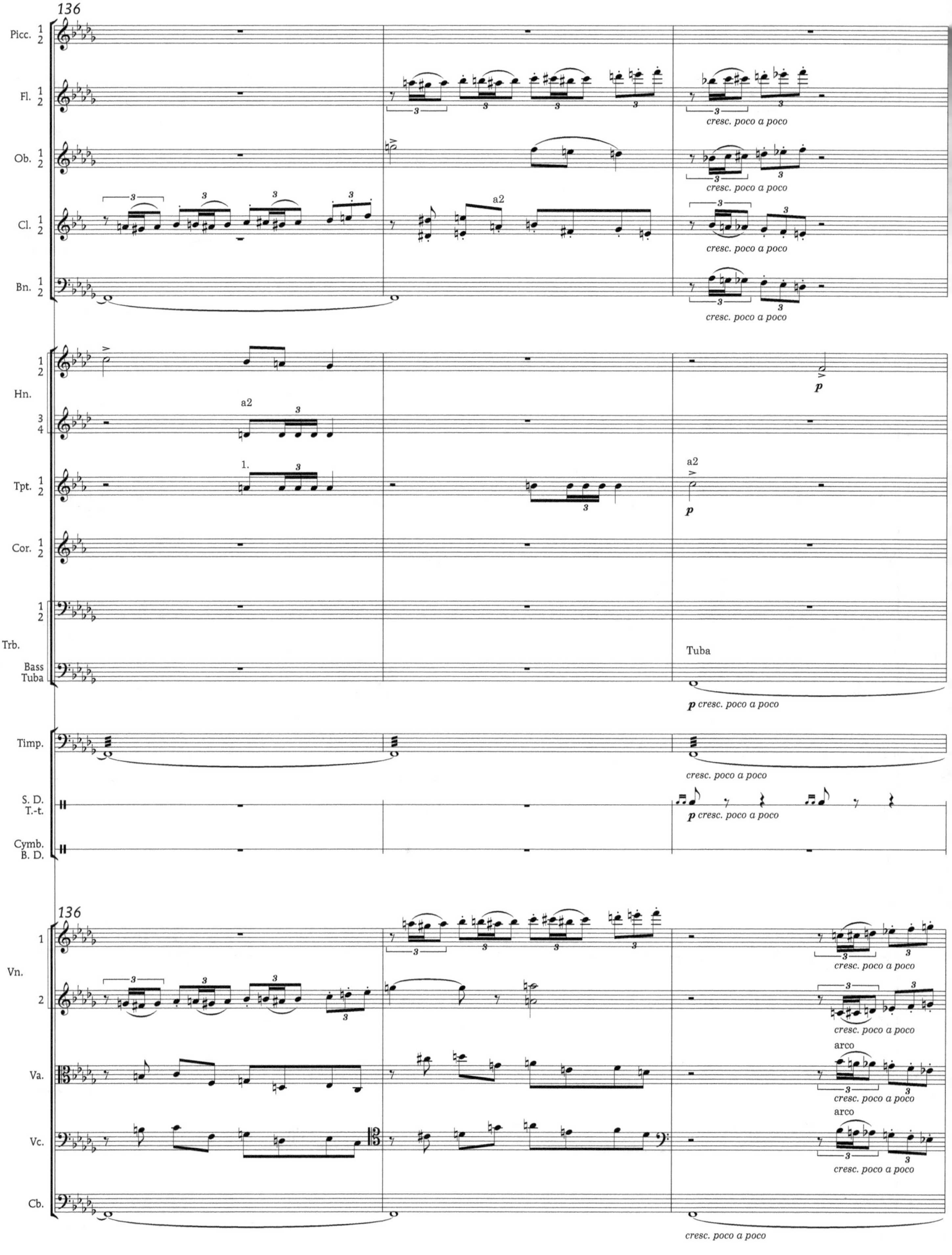

139
Picc. 1 2
Fl. 1 2
Ob. 1 2
Cl. 1 2
Bn. 1 2
Hn. 1 2 3 4
Tpt. 1 2
Cor. 1 2
Trb. 1 2
Bass Tuba
Timp.
S. D. T.-t.
Cymb. B. D.
Vn. 1 2
Va.
Vc.
Cb.
più f
mf

142
Picc. 1 2
Fl. 1 2
Ob. 1 2
2.
Cl. 1 2
Bn. 1 2
Hn. 1 2 3 4
3.
a2
Tpt. 1 2
Cor. 1 2
Trb. 1 2
Bass Tuba
Timp.
S. D. T.-t.
Cymb. B. D.
142
Vn. 1 2
Va.
pizz.
arco
Vc.
Cb.

145
Picc. 1 2
Fl. 1 2
Ob. 1 2
Cl. 1 2
Bn. 1 2
Hn. 1 2 3 4
Tpt. 1 2
Cor. 1 2
Trb. 1 2
Bass Tuba
Timp.
S. D. T.-t.
Cymb. B. D.
Vn. 1 2
Va.
Vc.
Cb.
2.
a2
cresc.
f
fp
arco

147
Picc. 1 2
Fl. 1 2
Ob. 1 2
Cl. 1 2
Bn. 1 2
Hn. 1 2 3 4
Tpt. 1 2
Cor. 1 2
Trb. 1 2
Bass Tuba
Timp.
S. D. T.-t.
Cymb. B. D.
147
Vn. 1 2
Va.
Vc.
Cb.
f
ff

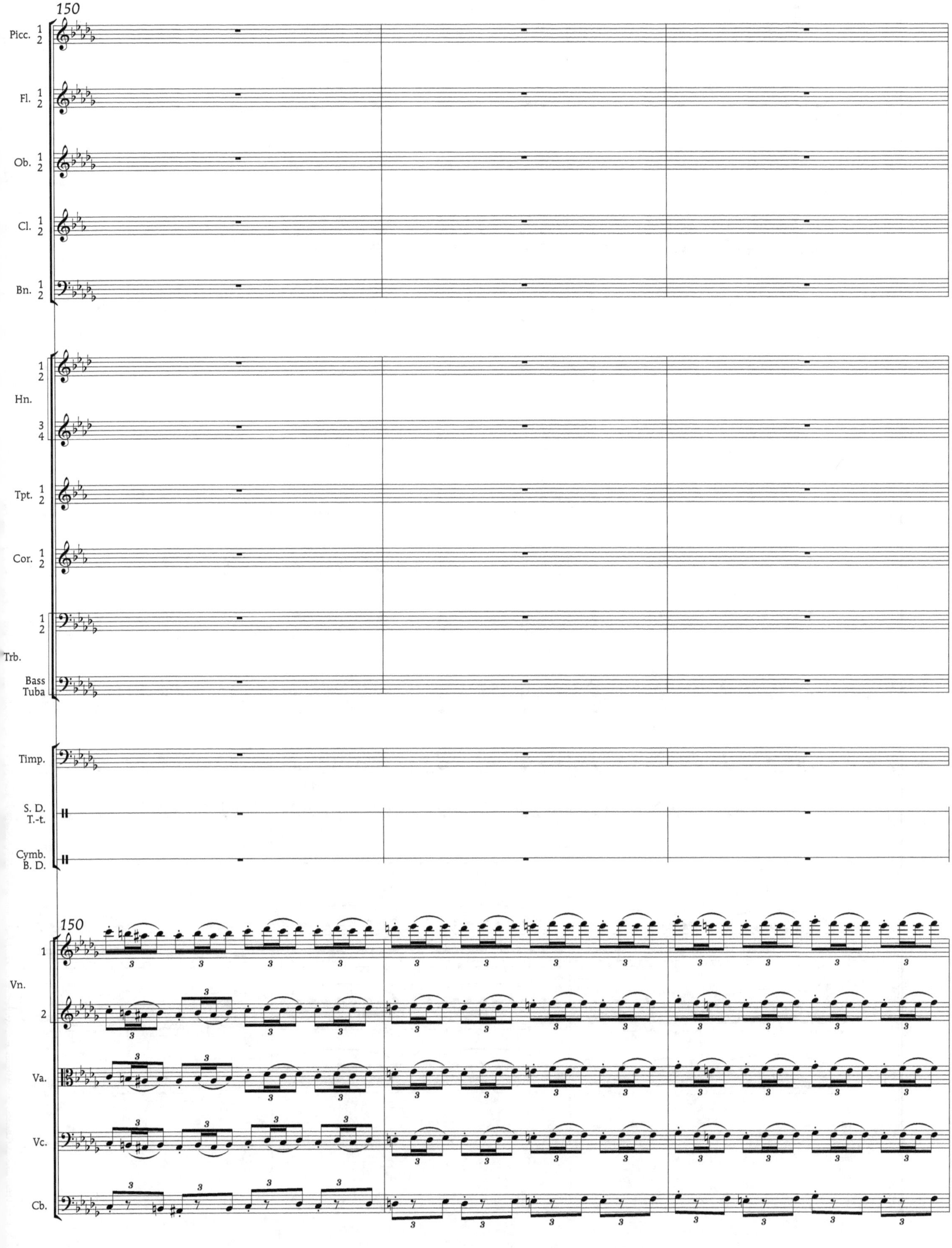
150
Picc. 1 2
Fl. 1 2
Ob. 1 2
Cl. 1 2
Bn. 1 2
Hn. 1 2 3 4
Tpt. 1 2
Cor. 1 2
Trb. 1 2
Bass Tuba
Timp.
S. D. T.-t.
Cymb. B. D.
150
Vn. 1 2
Va.
Vc.
Cb.

153
a2
Picc. 1 2
ff
Fl. 1 2
ff
a2
Ob. 1 2
ff marc.
Cl. 1 2
ff
Bn. 1 2
ff
a2
Hn. 1 2
ff marc.
a2
3 4
ff
a2
Tpt. 1 2
ff marc.
Cor. 1 2
ff
Trb. 1 2
ff
Bass Tuba
ff
Timp.
ff
S. D. T.-t.
ff
Cymb. B. D.
153
Vn. 1
2
Va.
Vc.
marc.
Cb.

156
Picc. 1 2
Fl. 1 2
Ob. 1 2
Cl. 1 2
Bn. 1 2
Hn. 1 2
3 4
Tpt. 1 2
Cor. 1 2
Trb. 1 2
Bass Tuba
Timp.
S. D. T.-t.
Cymb. B. D.
156
Vn. 1
2
Va.
Vc.
Cb.

159
Picc.
Fl.
Ob.
Cl.
Bn.
Hn.
Tpt.
Cor.
Trb.
Bass Tuba
Timp.
S. D. T.-t.
Cymb. B. D.
Vn.
Va.
Vc.
Cb.
a2
fff

163
Picc. 1 2
Fl. 1 2
Ob. 1 2
Cl. 1 2
Bn. 1 2
Hn. 1 2
3 4
Tpt. 1 2
Cor. 1 2
Irb. 1 2
Bass Tuba
Timp.
S. D. T.-t.
Cymb. B. D.
163
Vn. 1
2
Va.
Vc.
Cb.

*While not in the manuscript, most likely left out by mistake

172
Picc. 1 2
Fl. 1 2
Ob. 1 2
Cl. 1 2
Bn. 1 2
Hn. 1 2
3 4
Tpt. 1 2
Cor. 1 2
Trb. 1 2
Bass Tuba
Timp.
S. D. T.-t.
Cymb. B. D.
172
Vn. 1
2
Va.
Vc.
Cb.

175
Picc. 1 2
Fl. 1 2
Ob. 1 2
Cl. 1 2
Bn. 1 2
Hn. 1 2 3 4
Tpt. 1 2
Cor. 1 2
Trb. 1 2
Bass Tuba
Timp.
S. D. T.-t.
Cymb. B. D.
175
Vn. 1 2
Va.
Vc.
Cb.
arco
arco
f
mf
p

179
Picc. 1 2
Fl. 1 2
Ob. 1 2
Cl. 1 2
p
1.
Bn. 1 2
p
Hn. 1 2 3 4
Tpt. 1 2
Cor. 1 2
Trb. 1 2
Bass Tuba
Timp.
S. D. T.-t.
Cymb. B. D.
179
Vn. 1 2
Va.
Vc.
arco
Cb.

187 **più mosso. Allegro**

184

Picc. 1 2

Fl. 1 2

Ob. 1 2

Cl. 1 2

Bn. 1 2

Hn. 1 2

Hn. 3 4

Tpt. 1 2

Cor. 1 2

Trb. 1 2

Bass Tuba

Timp.

S. D. T.-t.

Cymb. B. D.

187 **più mosso. Allegro**

184

Vn. 1

Vn. 2

Va.

Vc.

Cb.

191
Picc. 1 2
Fl. 1 2
Ob. 1 2
Cl. 1 2
Bn. 1 2
mf
1.
mf
Hn. 1 2
3 4
Tpt. 1 2
Cor. 1 2
Trb. 1 2
Bass Tuba
Timp.
poco più f
S. D. T.-t.
p
Cymb. B. D.
191
pizz.
p
Vn. 1
2
pizz.
p
Va.
Vc.
poco più f
Cb.
poco più f

195
Picc. 1 2
Fl. 1 2
Ob. 1 2
Cl. 1 2
Bn. 1 2
Hn. 1 2 3 4
Tpt. 1 2
Cor. 1 2
Trb. 1 2
Bass Tuba
Timp.
S. D. T.-t.
Cymb. B. D.
195
Vn. 1 2
Va.
Vc.
Cb.
arco
f

199
Picc. 1 2
Fl. 1 2
ff
Ob. 1 2
f
Cl. 1 2
ff
Bn. 1 2
ff
2.
Hn. 1 2
mf
a2
3 4
f
1.
Tpt. 1 2
f
Cor. 1 2
1 2
Trb.
Tuba
Bass Tuba
mf
Timp.
mf
S. D. T.-t.
mf
Cymb. B. D.
199
arco
Vn. 1
f
2
f
arco
Va.
f
Vc.
f
Cb.
f

203
Picc. 1 2
Fl. 1 2
Ob. 1 2
Cl. 1 2
Bn. 1 2
fff
Hn. 1 2
3 4
Tpt. 1 2
Cor. 1 2
ff
a2
Trb. 1 2
Bass Tuba
Timp.
S. D. T.-t.
Cymb. B. D.
Vn. 1
2
div.
Va.
Vc.
Cb.

207
Picc. 1 2
Fl. 1 2
Ob. 1 2
Cl. 1 2
Bn. 1 2
Hn. 1 2 3 4
Tpt. 1 2
Cor. 1 2
fff
Trb. 1 2
a2
Bass Tuba
Timp.
S. D. T.-t.
Cymb. B. D.
207
Vn. 1 2
Va.
Vc.
Cb.

213 **Andante molto maestoso**

213 **Andante molto maestoso**

*manuscript Bass Drum has beats
3 & 4 same rhythm as beats 1 & 2

** Flutes 1 and 2 pitches are
reversed in the manuscript

218
Picc. 1 2
Fl. 1 2
Ob. 1 2
Cl. 1 2
Bn. 1 2
Hn. 1 2 3 4
Tpt. 1 2
Cor. 1 2
Trb. 1 2
Bass Tuba
Timp.
S. D. T.-t.
Cymb. B. D.
218
Vn. 1 2
Va.
Vc.
Cb.

Allegro risoluto

Allegro risoluto

224
a2
a2
Picc. 1 2
Fl. 1 2
Ob. 1 2
Cl. 1 2
Bn. 1 2
Hn. 1 2 3 4
Tpt. 1 2
Cor. 1 2
Trb. 1 2
Bass Tuba
Timp.
S. D. T.-t.
Cymb. B. D.
224
Vn. 1 2
Va.
Vc.
Cb.

233
229
Picc. 1 2
Fl. 1 2
Ob. 1 2
Cl. 1 2
Bn. 1 2
Hn. 1 2 3 4
Tpt. 1 2
Cor. 1 2
Trb. 1 2
Bass Tuba
Timp.
S. D. T.-t.
Cymb. B. D.
233
229
Vn. 1 2
Va.
Vc.
Cb.

234
Picc. 1 2
Fl. 1 2
Ob. 1 2
Cl. 1 2
Bn. 1 2
Hn. 1 2 3 4
Tpt. 1 2
Cor. 1 2
Trb. 1 2
Bass Tuba
Timp.
S. D. T.-t.
Cymb. B. D.
234
Vn. 1 2
Va.
Vc.
Cb.

238
a2
Picc. 1 2
Fl. 1 2
Ob. 1 2
Cl. 1 2
Bn. 1 2
Hn. 1 2
3 4
Tpt. 1 2
Cor. 1 2
Trb. 1 2
Bass Tuba
Timp.
S. D.
T.-t.
Cymb.
B. D.
Vn. 1
2
Va.
Vc.
Cb.

64

248
Picc. 1 2
Fl. 1 2
a2
Ob. 1 2
Cl. 1 2
Bn. 1 2
Hn. 1 2 3 4
Tpt. 1 2
Cor. 1 2
Trb. 1 2
Bass Tuba
Timp.
S. D. T.-t.
Cymb. B. D.
Vn. 1 2
Va.
Vc.
Cb.

252
Picc. 1 2
Fl. 1 2
Ob. 1 2
Cl. 1 2
Bn. 1 2
Hn. 1 2 3 4
Tpt. 1 2
Cor. 1 2
Trb. 1 2
Bass Tuba
Timp.
S. D. T.-t.
Cymb. B. D.
Vn. 1 2
Va.
Vc.
Cb.
fff

256
Picc. 1 2
Fl. 1 2
Ob. 1 2
Cl. 1 2
a2
Bn. 1 2
Hn. 1 2
3 4
Tpt. 1 2
a2
Cor. 1 2
a2
Trb. 1 2
a2
Bass Tuba
Timp.
S. D. T.-t.
Cymb. B. D.
256
Vn. 1
2
Va.
Vc.
Cb.

www.ingramcontent.com/pod-product-compliance
Lightning Source LLC
LaVergne TN
LVHW061340060426
835511LV00014B/2029